TECHNICAL SOLACE

Rebecca G. Biber

FIFTH
AVENUE
PRESS

CONTENTS

ACKNOWLEDGMENTS

I would like to thank the Ann Arbor Writers Group for their helpful criticism and camaraderie. Several poems in this collection were inspired by other works of art, so I would like to acknowledge the fine work done by the Wild Swan Theater company in their production of *The Firebird*, an adaptation of the Russian classic; and by the University of Michigan School of Music, Theatre & Dance in its production of the play *Eurydice*, a modern retelling of the ancient Greek myth, by Sarah Ruhl. More generally, I wish to acknowledge the significance of music school in my thinking. The original version of "Idyll" was written on the lawn of the School between classes. "Ode to the Violin" owes its inspiration to my strings colleagues, who I hope are still playing. "Heiligenstadt" is a student's meditation on a past master. Many of the other poems reference the piano or music in general. Relatedly, I thank the editors of the forthcoming *Bop, Strut, and Dance* anthology, Afaa Michael Weaver and Tara Betts, for the contest that inspired "Carry it to the Captain" and various other poems based on African American songs and musical forms.

Thanks to Sara Talpos and Bets Davies, both early and astute readers. Thanks to my family and good friends for tolerating being written about and offering nothing but encouragement.

Finally, my gratitude to the staff of the Ann Arbor District Library, who made this book real and readable. Sherlonya Turner and Erin Helmrich guided me through manuscript submission; Amanda Szot and Tom Smith are graphical geniuses; and Chris Porter oversaw everything. Working with you has been a rare privilege.

A Y E

Always want to cry, I
always want to laugh, I'm like
those two drama masks: rage
and rictus, lozenge eyes.
Sometimes ribbons
get attached. Always
want to speak, want to hide
not knowing if I know
the answer or besides, which
question, assuming they
bother to ask, listen
before voting nay.

BIRD I

Resting, roosting, or dying, the mourning
dove stays on the deck all day. Gears
up to flap, to fly, can't
get any height. Running, grubbing
she's good at, she's got. One wing
sits funny at the rear, fletched
like an amateur arrow. Oh sky.
She flutters a few inches. She struts
my boards, seeking exit. Regards me
with one onyx eye. She knows out
is up but the lift won't take. Again, false
starts. Again, impatient pacing, as if why.

BIRD II

She's the color of dusk
from dun beak to grey tail tip
her black jewel eye
tracks me until I go inside
as dark comes on, she fades
into—or it fades into her.
I don't know if she will live
the night. This morning
she wasn't mine to care
how shades of buff, beige
brown and bruise
fill the evening's hollow
feathered air.

P I E D   P I P E R

It took me a while to catch on
N.B. meant no breath, not
nota bene. Eighth notes
should flow uphill as though charmed.
It took me until reading age to see
mark my words in folk tales and not
hear *mock*, the way characters talked
onstage, on screen. Ye olden
accent. Commit to memory,
            note well.

I began playing the flute because of a man
in tricorn hat on TV. My college
vibrato stopped at the hasped door of
intimidation. Last chair.

In every story there's the clever part
and the brave. The smart hero can remember,
unclasp the code, discern the trail. (*Know
your motivic sequence from your phrase.*) The brave
(derring-do or *Daring, do!*) would throw
the precious object, smite the king, run toward,
not away from, flames. Sit down at the banquet of a hundred
choices and not choose.
Touch nothing.

It took me all the tales until right now: don't
            breathe. Don't clip that thread of make-
believe. If you are clever
and brave enough, mock my words, you will succeed.

SPANISH

It is evening all day, storms
loom un-secretly on the radar. Lorca,
my high school hero, wrote green
how I love you green. Those years
it was evening, Sunday evening, in my
heart all the time. Work was no comfort,
play was an artifact, the only help
words like a necklace beginning and ending
at the clasp of that idea, colorful shimmer in
an otherwise blotted scene. The man who died
young and tragically as every high school
hero should, incantatory list of horse, tree, girl,
caught in the persistent, cistern-filling rain. It rained
through his pages as it rained in my head. Today
I wish Lorca had grown old to become
banal, like me. It is Monday morning
and chores wait for no lament. Outside
clouds are traveling their straight line in.

LAZY MONEY

The fund that no one spends or disperses,
that takes in interest where its berth is:
the lazy money.
She won't be squandered or sundered;
she's the good you don't throw after bad.
She pulls the blanket to her chin,
rolls over another quarter,
the account unplundered,
a sweet naïf who won't be had.
She consents to no barter, no purchase.
She's the daughter who turns from the party
to ask where the church is.

GANGA

Imagine a river falling to earth
splashing caught in the hammock of a man's hair

Her hugeness, life of flood and monsoon
lithe as a five-foot ballerina

Nothing is fixed, the nature of woman
or world, some surges do not start from below

She woke happy and graceful having been washwater
the night before. She got up and danced in white silk.

Nothing is preordained, the river's presence
or man's, fidelity in marriage,

she had to be coaxed, had to consent, small
smile and hands like reeds spinning questions.

When she descends hilly clouds, casually
spilled from a god's canteen, imagine

thirst so urgent it turns spirits mortal. Maybe
the fall made her more holy, not less

her belief in a couple's firm heels striking
the dusty path together, throwing out white buds

from black hair, being both ordinary and a river.
Perhaps he caught her with his mind.

MEMENTO MORI

The objects you give me
fade. They don't
break or get
jammed in drawers; I cease
to see them, merely.
Were you and I
to quit today—calm
discussion or tandem
tantrum, either way—
these things would
turn visible
quick. I'd enter a
room previously dull
and see, clearly as if
it came alive
and told me off, the thick
ceramic rose and,
risible almost, glass
animals I planned to
fold into your palm
in the full gloom
of avoided spats,
assuming
we'd proceed
as, in fact, we have.

A SOUVENIR OF YOUR SECOND YEAR

for S.A.L.

Luckily we forget the pain of teething:
reluctant letting-through of dull
molars that gums do,
and the press of swollen sinus
against the skull.
It's good we let that go, apprehending bright,
vivid memories that impress
more deeply. It's a shame, though,
we also forget, with no more
knowledge of the loss than a child
sleepily letting go conscious thought,
the feeling of flight
or floating gently tethered, aquarium sound
surrounding us day and night
in the womb.
What is too early to remember,
what gets lost in birth, waking,
and glorious baths of light
is the euphoria before breathing:
the painless mouth,
the perfect slumber.

THE CHILDREN'S *FIREBIRD*

That she is red no one would
argue. A young viewer suggests
a superhero. Meaning she can't
be killed by guns or time, only
recast all her life. The word thrall.

The hands' movement over rounded
air, the stepstones made by speech
(your mouth, my ear). Have you seen
or have you known? "He brought
a wineskin filled with water."

It's not a trope, that all demons
are the same or close enough to be
played by one actor. That boots
make you taller. That mazes are
women. The abyss of the word abyss.

The way we've all met before, wolf
and hero, servant, translator, ogre,
mother, fate. The shining souvenir
from the bird's own body. The gesture
of dancing away from chains. The fear.

OTHER TRIBE

There was the swart face reflected in clear water
gazing on its own image because no one owned
the place. Spreading wide.

Here is the pale face in the dream of red
setting custom aside as if only one side
knew the rules. And when I wake,

full of explanations and rebuttal
here is the fighting, there the wars already fought.
The framed visage of a bulletless soldier.

Here are the federal grants
too little to stanch a river of loss, standing
as markers on the falsehood road;

the totem outside City Hall, a benefit
concert on a generous guy's largesse
and other petite guilty obsequies;

Here is the fashion of fry bread and braids,
anthropomorphic moose whose antlers
point to the spirit-dotted sky.

When I sleep, the dead hold me to a harsh light
asking about the smallpox when they were small,
grasping with fingers like straw.

Here is the landing shore of another fleeing people
who got here too late to help, and sing latent
wordless chants for the slaughter already done.

AWAY, RUSSIA

"Heat the samovar...
why do you stand at the door?
Let's not behave like Gentiles."
—*Lomir Zikh Iberbetn* (Let's Make Up)

We left as if voluntarily
looking back only once.
We came to criticize and improve,
learning English better than you.
Took note of black people.

We left without a primer, knowing
merely your doffing of hats.
We arrived sewn full of ritual, permitted at last
the luxury of wasted water.
Never got the hang of plastic wrap.

We came with braided candles
and pomaded thick hair.
We entered America, that vast simcha,
clapping as if we knew the rhythm,
hurtling forward on the syllables of our good names.

DOTTY

So you've killed the nemesis
of a charming people... The Wichita
Hallmark would've had a card for that. The trouble
with greeting cards is they can't be self-administered,
         ditto awards, plaques, recognition of any kind. Great.

         Didn't we want to stay supine in
the poppies, stretching only to reset the alarm? Dream
within a dream. And what would be the harm?

         Fire
        ˙and water
         are getting so tired.
         Someone please grab an extinguisher
         -and- extinguish 'er. That's great. Powerful
         stuff.

The city is jewels but I just want my
Yorkie back. Someone please. He hasn't been microchipped
yet. And won't they shut up with their *Oh*s and *Ah*s, easily
amazed and easily fazed. I'd be glad not to see
or hear anything of Ahs ever again.

ENGLISH

I needed jokes to be
explained. I analyzed cartoons. Scary
things thrilled me and everything
was scary. I needed a docent in
life to steer me around the
unseeable, intuit when I cried
at the sight of our kindly neighbor
walking by, I thought Mr. Wulff
was the wolf from the story, to give
full exegesis of the English show
where the guy in bandages tries to
scare his friend but the friend isn't
scared: I needed to know how fear
could be turned off like lights. With
a clever word, something you taught
me, a pun. How play fright could stay
play. Needed the world translated,
printed in a widely-spaced left-handed
set, worded for safety the same
way you explained me to myself.
The drawings were rough, voices
dubbed by the animator's son. So simple
and corny now: a yellow flashlight beam,
an initial gasp, then the line "a very nice mummy."
There are only two things this could mean.

MINIATURE

I can't let go of her
to write: length
of my forearm, soft black
baguette, aging with every
happy breath. I memorialize
in advance.
       This elegy has no deadline
       and death has no
       recompense. She is a dog.
My life is long. Her devotion is
specific but pervasive, like an ink
cloud spreading from a single drop.
My job is to take care, broadly,
the small beast
alert when I wake
       (walks, medicine, play, respite)
companion of my sleep, slight
weight against my hip.

She's here as I anticipate
her gone. My job
is to cede control, briefly,
short hairs over her neck
cresting, falling back.
She licks my hand because
it tastes good. Salt
to her is never a sad thing
       but I guard my weeping
       with the stupid strength
       of a god.
I can't let go of her to cry.

BAD INFLUENCES

I can see the trees at the back of the house, yellow
for one more week before it's all a pool of tiger butter
on the ground. Pancakes sound good. I don't wish
to offend the reader, it's pancakes I thought of holding
or having narrated to me the racist picture book.

    Well-fed and well read, many's the night I too dreamed
of cheese, toasted, mostly. Marooned in bed. Was there violence
on Treasure Island? Cutlasses.

    The scent of sausages, their crispy sound that you don't
really hear in a Jewish house came through the wooden caravan
of Danny and his dad, poaching pheasants and only many chapters
later did it come to light that Dahl, that Scandinavian, was
an anti-Semite. Who rooted for clever underdogs. I could go on:
Huck, Tom, Caddie Woodlawn afraid of nothing except the brown
skins.
All that came fluttering down on my head, so if anyone
tried to take my books would I have stood there, stunned?
Or grabbed, hit back, run to my room? Now some claim
stories as bad influences, undercut the brain. But
my folks poured tomes and tales over us like leaves, made us
rake, helped us haul out words and worth; now I can see the trees
through the open front door, past the shoes and notions I keep
by the back door, sliding glass closed to frame ocher and orange,
yes—they are the ones I love, far as they are, far older
than this page. I used to meet friends, victims, the hard and down
on their luck, the ones who stuck their necks out before I was born,
I read the food and colors, cackles, hatbands, watching the great yard
out there, house between, house not going anywhere, I could burn through
a book a day, holes in the roof be damned.

INDIRECT APPROACH APPROACH

Better to come at it
from the side, the way
it comes at us: one second
there is a flower or a
moth (hovering around
a flower) the next second
we're thinking big
spirits, vast. Tree-size
sky-size, unimpeachable
spirits.

      Whereas
if we start from universal
eternal, how will we ever
get back to us or that
moth or that flower?

FOR MY
EX-BOYFRIENDS' FAMILIES

For Phil, whose black-and-white
photographs were each a small country
with an unknown history; for Anne Catherine,
who cried when Chuck said he was an atheist.
For Don, whose sailor beard and rough hands
belied a modern humor.

For the smart sisters and dumb brothers-in-law,
for the parents of relations I met only once
who used to live around the corner from where I now live,
before I lived there. For Grant,
with his purse,
and Sarah, with her tiny purple hearing aids,
scooping in the sand.

For the now-wives, who happily took my place
and their preacher uncles, who officiated.

For the sexy male cousin
I wanted slightly more;
for the grandmother I couldn't break
up with, the siblings who claimed me for life, the folks
who said don't let
her get away. I got away.

For Emily, if that is still her name
and gender. For William, who never
changes. For Sue, who said gosh.
For Sergio, who did not cry or get angry
when Chuck announced his atheism,

and for Chuck, who still answers phones at the church.

WINTER'S FOOL
April, Ann Arbor, 2014

It resembles spring, that's as good as I can give you.
It's not snowing at the moment, and the ban on marriage
lifted last night. Temporarily, say. It's still cold
and windy out there. My row of tulips, sheltered halfway
behind boxwoods, is getting intrepidly up but tomorrow
the old governor might stop the process again; we'll find
discouraged flowers ice-rimed and separated pairs of men. On
the road, asphalt looks like gold. We wait to change tires, clothes,
hold out hope, until sure the sleet has gone, fled in drops and shiny
rivulets down drains tucked under curbs. We halt, wary of pride, Michigan
tough and winter tender, hoisting signs: *Love is love,* as jays meander
back to the trees they dwell in. Bold nature says, "of course I'm here,
where else?" Each frail fellow creature without a house or car, feral,
fearless as humans wish to be. We move from desk to store to bedroom,
from van to school to kitchen, wincing to be caught between. We move
from habit to decision back to routine, until today. Maybe just
this day, a line at the county clerk's office and flowers in women's hands.
The freezing-out cannot be ended, it's too unlikely, I don't trust
the reprieve. But for now. When my boot goes through
the ice, not over. When one bit of good news is on the radio every hour.
When we linger on the pavement around the store, when mail carriers
again are glad they hired on, rain and color stand a chance, chapped lips
heal and debates resume, when the art class sees the jay, the branch, picks
up pencils and moves outside for drawing, it resembles spring, resembles
something thawing.

ARTICHOKE

We go cataloguing
each what the other says
things like artichoke
is a cold weather food and I
shaved my beard at the photographer's.
We trust the details, cross-
hatching and hoarding our days.

Meanwhile Marie looks skyward,
oceanward, inward, dismissing
debris. She builds up her interlocking
boys with a sandstone faith still warm
and granular to the touch—it shelters
her head and theirs and desert plants
grow in its shade.

I D Y L L

The hill careers to the pond without rest, a scrub
of cattails obscures the drop; midday colors
perform a test: my faith in their bright
veracity. A man-made fountain spits.
Reading the paper, I'm drenched in the guile
and ruthlessness of crooks: child seller, janjaweed,
the murderer who, in his mendacity,
does it with a smile. My vision battles the article
before me; why hasn't the world gone still?

In shock, the fountain surely wants to stop
and, on the lawn, ducks and dogs call a halt
to their fighting, finding fault only
with the shortness of sunny hours. I could wrap
myself in willow branches, obscured. If everyone
paused for breath, would it help?
I tremble to the pond without ceasing or slowing
my stride, wet my feet near the redwing and weeds,
think better and retreat.

I'll bring a camera next time and record
ducks, dogs, steadfast trees, delirious green and
yellow harsh as screaming, let the image skip around,
changing from what men do to what the sun
sees: we all crave rest. Rows of reeds are merely
clamoring for peace. Nothing lasts, however good
or bad; worlds crack in two, revealing
other spheres. They show our own
decease. The crime reporter drowns me in his tears.

INTERNAL

If the door closes I am lost.
Your eyes have a secret hallway
where I am not yet allowed
to touch a thing.
On a table in the hallway
lies a crumbling photograph
the same sepia
as your iris.
If I look too hard
I will burn the picture.
If I speak too loudly
my breath will close the door.

CARRY IT TO THE CAPTAIN

Your pickax and hammer are hard artifacts
like chitin—the lowly bug's armor and implement—
and, sloughed off, make you an escapee, quick-
crawling toward next season. I'll get there in lots
more time, underfed. I'll take your task
and add it to mine; goodbye and don't blame me
the heavy load. I know, the way work and forced work
look the same but feel so different hurt your pride.

I am hungry, helpful and caught. Farewell, don't grudge
the moment you saw my eyes and knew I'd stay.
I stay for you. You go for me. Acres of parched
earth and the things it grows or kills interpolate. Mud,
green shoots, grey rock, soles of your feet, try
sprinting in this rhythm: if he should ask   you
          was I laughin
you can tell him I was cryin.

Somebody has to carry and explain, somebody
has to sing the outcome. I'm Horatio
cleaning up after Hamlet; the bard at Troy; factotum
barbiere della città, famous in my own mouth. A song
we used to labor to haunts my ease. I wake and pause,
bearing these tools and this news, and if he should ask   me
          were you runnin
I can tell him you were flyin.

Q W E R T Y

After we saw the old black typewriter in the shop's
musty back, red keys arrayed in stadium steps
gleaming, just dusted (you clacked out "leaves of grass"
below the bar: the sound of railroad tracks)
I told you the tale, how qwerty came to be,

how someone had to stop the secretaries'
fast hands, their lady fingers, slack word speed
that jammed mere metal, crossed levers, broke
one against the other. For progress, men
rearranged the letters. Then driving home

on the highway between two fast food towns we saw
the corn in hill-combed rows: silk tops, rustling green-
bottomed swell. White signs sold stories of a new
pesticide, built in the vegetables'
inside, that, when eaten, should go down fine.

This kind of scarecrow maddens. We glanced away
and men rearranged the kernels. We were working,
machines could not keep up, the body ecstatic,
obsolete. Another industrial fancy
to make you miss Walt Whitman and John Henry.

LITTLE PORTRAIT

Love rules love
rocks, your mind
un-hardened by
heart. Love schooled
will, its wont.
She's in she's
great, your granddaughter,
essentially smart. She's
you, son love, the matter,
the mind, involuntary
jewel. She is art
without trying, dewdrops
on lips, human
bloom, mouth open
to the mothering world.

CLASSICAL

The letters chrysanthemum
don't mean petals any more
than clock means time

or lake, mirror. Apt
placeholders for each other,
objects inelegant, pure:

wave contains but isn't
heave and swell, nor chimes
the hour, the word bloom

essence of a pale pink—what is pink?—flower.

LOCATIONAL SELF-PORTRAIT

Arriving in loud, a land
I'm not at home in, and denizens
know it, how can I blend, abroad
in timbre, tumbled in motley
pitch? Bound for bewilderment
I find a hands-breadth of space
to be mute a sec.

This is the norm, with effort: speak
harshly, act for big effect. The rule
is broad strokes, crude. My native
tongue is better for detail than
amplitude; thoughts hold pleasure—
color, design—more than
their drowning would.

We may all be born into
loud, little ears unstrained by
our own dire wails, but I've no memory
of being fine with stridency. Human
noise: I love the moment it
breaks, my breath-intake as
it dissipates.

I will dwell in quiet, or relative,
edges frayed, having left loud
long since, where I failed to disguise
my taste for subtle accents—eyebrows
super high to compensate my wince—
some kind of sonic polyglot, immigrant,
unnaturalized.

VISITORS

Last night it was a fox
fox-colored, fox-like but big
as a bus; all I had was an umbrella and
a glass table to bang it against. I woke
up. Sometimes it's a snake
snake-colored, snake-like but fangs
the size of kitchen knives. Every night
it's an animal; it's never a man. It's never
a warlord. It's never Hitler. It's never the
boyfriend who threatened to rape me because
he thought I enjoyed talk like that
until I woke up.

HEILIGENSTADT

"...and yet it was impossible for me to say to men, 'Speak louder, shout,
for I am deaf.'"
—L. van Beethoven, October 6, 1802

The green reminds me how well I can see
which reminds me how poorly I hear; the sun
prickles the eczema under my linen sleeves. Have begun
feeling like selfish Papa, which reminds me of the boys.
Boys, keep my things without quarreling and, when
necessary, sell them, though security in this life
cannot be bought. Nor can it be earned.

Vienna watches from an hour's ride off, how I spent
the bright day, sketchbooks filling like a cistern, head
full of intervals. The first one: genesis of a tune like grey
dawn. When exactly was the last note I heard? City
dwellers expect output and fail to fathom high
loneliness, the empty jar of pomade I won't
replace, since women will not be coming here, not her.

They refuse to know me. So I refuse to explain. Perhaps
I hide behind temper, the document my sanguine
confidante. I will return after the long rest's duration,
brush the way smooth with apology; they'll smile, forget
to ask about those clefless days and pages. Time never
got away from me. I will keep on knocking at the gates
of joy and her heart, feeling volume through my damaged palms.

S T I L L / S T E E L

How long since I was galvanized
more than a bucket you drop wet clay into
content with the job of receiving, the fate
of holding was it the time I performed
(if anything's external it's a concert) on the piano
manufacturing ropes of notes and their meanings if they
have meanings sending the audience out with parcels
of sound or was it that earlier time I first put words with
music and thought I could do this however much
or little length I am given and brightly, with no sense
of the space below me stepped onto the plank of a stage and into
the woven metal trap of a microphone? Who was she? I've lost my when.

REMEDY

The way poetic feet sound like
torso terms. Amphibrachic, tachycardia,
trochaic, bradyarrhythmia. A murmur, a
slowness or skip. Could my chest scan
keep me pacing, will your investigation
into its beats
clear up
anything?
It's a waltz, not a bird, the dactyl. It's a
shove, not a bother, anapest. Not a plate
of meat and cheese, syllables such
as these.

BLUE AND WHITE

Imagine coming here from France: Provence,
Auvergne were never like this, countryside
of painted steel and nothing growing. Kids
say shoulda went, accrost and ain't
while parents do their best not to get
yelled at by the guy in charge today: the boss,
God maybe. Blue and white halls of school,
plant and church all cinderblock-made.

A traveler could walk out of the city
into this, dropping neatly off the world's
edge into anonymity, but the abyss holds
McDonald's and its knots of denizens.
Their paper-wrapped treats held in a fleeting
warm place. Their eyes on the walker-in.
I come from the university but might
be of an alien race; kids can smell
difference and their parents balk at means.

Try not to strike or be stricken here,
calm as the colors of an obsolete nation-state's
flag, full of warnings, low on help, best
equipped for a job opening this town won't have.

THIS IS ALL

The first few minutes of café window
warm on the inside, cold on the out-,
bright everywhere, you gaze on my mouth
having forgotten, thoughts ablaze,
I seemed beautiful for weeks, awhile

but not enduringly. The smile
loses its effect and coffee takes
over: redolence, remembrance of why
we were never lovers—no way
for you to detect the sweet gravity

beneath my immoderate laugh and,
for me, disappointment of watching
eyes mannered at the lashes, bored
otherwise. This is all the reason
I need to go home alone, goodbye

to plate glass, fixed grin, black beans
poured over ice or heated to steaming.
Tonight my hair kept the smell of spice
and I found the encounter's punchline:
your doubt was my redeeming.

SLIPPING

Pride
like ice
goes before a fall
the one your fault
the other wrought by winter.
Ice will melt
and bruised thighs
grow sound again.
Not everything heals—
does hurt pride rely
too much
on the perceived slight?
A hard thing to evaluate
when you feel
half of life is ice
disguised
its contrast with firm ground
too light to see
the other half a spring grown warm
and kind if rather late.

EURYDICE HALFWAY
after Sarah Ruhl

Dad was already in the land of the dead
surprised when I arrived. He drew me
out of the boat, took my case, and tried
persistently to warm my hands with air.
Shuffled his feet. Humming of fluorescent
lights, or telephone wire. I felt bad,
wished to accommodate him, like I was
older and previously there.

What to say to my ghost progenitor
in fedora and rumpled suit? There is no
weather. I don't remember a thing,
but these talking rocks spit lies, I tell you what.
What if we both know one idea this minute
and it makes us strange? The man
bowed and angered me; like him I
wouldn't opt to forget.

That's life, he says, weak smile. It changes
according to rules I'd like to share
with you, if you don't mind. I know you're
a grown woman, but let me, honey, build
you this bedroom in Hell: paperclips and time.
Write letters, no one to stop
you trying. Keep out of the river.
Your young man waiting still.

O D E T O T H E V I O L I N

Non-musicians say "guiding
the bow over the strings" as if the bow
had its own life, only needed conveying and we,
not the instruments, were the solid pack animals, the
instruments, not ourselves, the wise conduits, cataloguers
of a thriving sound biology. We love that green reckoning where
science meets narration. We have always carried it on our backs, tired
at day's end. Perhaps the non-musicians are correct: the frogs and fingerboards
make decent masters. And tell me, which one of us shall last three hundred years?

SEVENTEEN

I used to find phantasmagoria in leaves
portents of collapse in strange
young men's sideways looks, it was
not the best of ages.

No one who loves seventeen
is seventeen. The smirk-and-glimmer
nostalgia is for forty or farther, back
then I was closer to death.

I left home to study music, I subscribed,
listened to everything said and sung,
respected the past despite its effrontery.
Never a very good year.

ON THE SAND

"Yo y mi sombra, ángulo recto.   *Me and my shadow, a right angle*
  Yo y mi sombra, libro abierto."   *Me and my shadow, an open book.*
    —Manuel Altolaguirre, "Playa"

You and your shadow, right and proper.
You and your shadow, innocuous, ready for reading.
You, maybe—the easy verse, bucolic
growth of people from landscape as if fused
by genes, sinews turned to tree roots in the sun. Boats
in pairs, yours because you saw them.

But your shadow? She is controlled by
circumstance, the time of day, direction the beach
stretches. If you wait until dusk
when she grows tall, slender and needy, or if the entire
panorama lifts itself and spins to face east,

it'll be you and your shadow, line without ending.
You and your shadow, sinister, merged.

CEMETERY I
for Dan, Gabe and Rachel

Names take many forms, some
English, some Hebrew. Behind
the laughing aloft baby, green
branches up, her arms insisting
alive, pond stones and fieldstones
line the marker's top.

These days upon leaving a grave
we Purell sanitize, the rest
is as a hundred years
before: the low wall of death,
a chubby infant in a cotton dress.
Israeli flags read the same front and back.

My new angle on stones
lying in the grass: each one is meant
for a person, now or sometime
and the trees overhead can't prevent
the old gate from opening
or our own flag from flying.

CEMETERY II
for John

We all like to think we're experts on our dads. Mostly it's true.
Anyone important? I ask: the photo is him holding you.
Same high waist, eyes straight at the lens,
liquor nowhere in view.

I'm a probationary student of my family, let alone yours.
There's a lot of comparing, chalking up, tallies I never verify.
How many parts mother and father could I be, and who
is the you of then? Did he die?

We all would know more about our lines; at times we can,
but pallbearing does not command your reverence.
Put her down in the hole, wearing stiff new cordovans,
shoes of memory snow-slick, casket handle
depending on the strength of other men.

ARCHITECT

In your mind there is one kind
of little girl: I am she
and she is her. This is why
you call my niece my name.

In our past it's just us
on the playground, incipient rain
leavening the clouds. Why I
think weather is partly father.

There's a gap in the record
book of our clan: I decided
no footnotes, no offspring. She
stands in. I'm yours, she's yours

But she's not mine. Knowledge
of how people are darkens her
brow. An old child. You two
alone, in the snow or leaves or sun.

TECHNICAL SOLACE

It was years before the scales became
like old jeans. The ease snuck
up on me, then there it was, keeping
me meditative in the afternoon. Sharps
made seams in smooth cloth, flicked
my fingers up and back. Those edges
led to Mozart, the iffy son.
        Arpeggios arrived
after, an unexpected second child
so squally I'd give up, surprised anytime
docility spread a smile. Tantrums
made me run outside, away from the
crying. But I always came back. Keys
are my landscape, cool barefoot
pedals like stones.

THE RUN OF A SHOW

Toward the end a hired hand
will pass up work for sleep and that's
not bad practice til taxes. In the middle,
ponder odd and even, when pay enters
the scene, where the extra dollar will be.
Check one, check two. Miss the cue
for Entr'acte, thinking of lucre. Before
money there was art; it was worth
asking if the actors like the music.
They drop a line and hurry the
dance, thinking of adulation.

ICE (PROMISES TO KEEP)

Like all adults, I didn't plan
to be this way. Worried speechless, snugged
by small creatures who seek comfort from me.
Like all teenagers I thought I'd hang on
to fantasy, the exception; my colors would stay
vivid, at least by moonlight. Like all kids, I knew
the hardest age to be was the one
I was, right then, each day.

Last night the pipes froze
but didn't break, and I'm singing
my mother's refrain: coulda been worse, coulda been...
In the mirror it's her over again, the strong
eyes, lips full of doubt. The oven still
cooks my food, furnace is nearly new.
The car has never not started. I wait for
that empty moment. I'm her age, I'm younger
than ever before, it's dark out and
thirteen below.

THE OPPOSITE OF SACAGAWEA
for N. and N.

Give the girl a gold coin.
It's good for kids to learn about
money, right, and trade it in. To have a face
with the name and number. In whom we trust.

Give her the powwow
regalia hand-made and beaded hour
by hour, the skirt's rows of fast added-up
stitches, shiny, hers until outgrown. The rest.

Sometimes the bank wins. No malice,
they just don't have the metal woman, only
him, paper like an old tarp, dark green and rank.
Here's the thrust: dismay is an erstwhile

reward. You ask for Sacagawea
and get Andrew Jackson. Perhaps he won't
make it onto Indian lands. Spend fives and tens
on what costs; give her herself for free, her pricelessness.

A GROOVE IN THE WOOD
December, 2012

The SWAT team stayed in my house all day, watching
through scopes for the man across the way to give
up, or allow police to coax him out and ask for
reasons, as if he knew. The one in charge, blue-toothed,
maybe forty-four, sat in my bedroom ("Call me Sarge"), broad
in the wood chair, gun atop a tripod on the chest where I store
extra blankets. Piercing winter sun made a good view
to that house where the man hunkered, perhaps armed. Gold
wreath on the green door: *céad míle fáilte* beneath.

Subordinate SWAT took the front room, young and huge,
straddled the piano bench, vast left boot leaving a weave
but not a speck of mud on the loomed rug. Would they have
to shoot? My silence; their answer offered anyhow: "We got
negotiators talking to him now, but if he's intent on killing
himself, it'd be moot." All day the contest of wills, my dog
nervous as I read and waited, shivering with the pass of cold
air through screens (not shooting my windows a top concern),
asking what was disturbed and what good, and who
controlled these hours. Evening came. The man
emerged, heavy, weary, half-lame from a rubber bullet. In the smooth
black wood of my piano bench, a slight groove where rifle butt
pressed harder than intended, the casual SWAT, young and deadly
kissing the air at my dog, only to stifle himself at radio crackle.
Only to fly out the door as the standoff ended. The commander
offered his thanks and moved my seat where it belonged, with
the instrument. The house was mine once more, is what I meant.

I'd gone pale around those weapons, now breathed again
at the close of a sluggish winter day, the bleak street
emptied of lights, cars and men and the neighbor's green door
with its hundred thousand welcomes closed, post-affray.

A SPECIAL AFFECTION FOR THE CHINESE GRANDMOTHERS

The ones whose sons teach at the engineering school,
whose daughters-in-law keep delivering these cute
babies (such an ugly baby). I see them strolling Green Road
in the fall sun, waiting for the bus, teaching toddlers stillness
under broad-brimmed hats. They learn, with the three-year-old
who points, which vehicle is mail truck, which neighbor is
African, how to avoid the lawn mower, not to eschew dogs. Evenings
after lessons they press homemade scallion pancakes into my
free hand and lay Ziplocs of red bean paste atop my briefcase. I see them
tilling without looking up the garden by the middle school that teenagers
should be weeding as I drive home. I used to walk through Sugarbush
in July to pick berries, and the Chinese grandmothers never
stared, only a few weeks later to pluck something like weeds
and stuff it into a paper bag. We get a few more of these placid
days, walking because we have the time, but work is turning
busy again, next year the baby will be in nursery, and as I pass
the raspberry vines at Green and Burbank I notice they're not
bearing anymore.

QUITS

I'm not equal to it usually
the sun rises and I'm still surprised.
What did you expect
        is the question when I talk bad clients
opening their doors antiseptic like I could contaminate
their living rooms and children, touching hands
and keys frankly with the proper name for all that
anatomy. What did I? Just that. The sad
and sour never take me aback, not as
they used to when I took the clouds for granted. Day
and night I look up, vastness
looks back with its firebird eye, turns me
inward, I'm not equal
        I'm greater than, less than, louder than
softer than, then uncaring, make me welcome
or turn me out, I've got the morning and the
next morning.

KEYBOARD RONDO III (ALBUMLEAF)

How many different saints you've been
and how often betrayed.
How various the kinds of din
you've borne in silent thought.
Each time I play, almost, a sin
and my damnation stayed
by your corrective mercy listening in.

Sometimes I cough up notes, as ill
as anyone who has bronchitis.
It shouldn't be like phlegm, or fill
my head with pounding pulse,
I know, and you remind me, still
upon your bench as Christ is
on his cross upon the hill.

Other days are better, the trill
tweedles out between lean fingers
that hardly seem mine, and no more will
is needed to play than desire.
Then all is temperate, nothing shrill
or gurbled, nothing lingers
after the pedal echoes to nil.

THE CALCULUS
OF POSSIBLE FINCHES

Usually it's mourning
doves but today
it's quick yellow tiny
darts of birds all gossiping three
five eight per branch as if the branches
flung them between, playing
bird-catch.

Are they finches? Not being a bird
taxonomist, I look them up. They
flee: flock or hyperbola
in space? Not knowing their calculus.

Do they recognize each other
one by one? Often I love
a man but today his heart is outside,
trying to stay warm in a feather-light
coat. Is it ennui, migration, are we listening

to chatter? Not owning binoculars
I see what I see. Leaving
the house, yard for a season or
forever could be chance
collectivity an asymptote or the desire to plummet alone.

TROMPE L'OEIL

Musée du Louvre, June,
my twenty-first year. I saw
Artemis, Pegasus, Napoleon's seat for three,
Jean d'Arc hearing voices, and a free
restroom, the only one so far.
Then there were the figures of the crypt,
full-length sculptures pilfered from catacombs:
some noble and his wife Robine.
I clung to her name,

peering at her greenish marble face.
I, too, want to lie atop my last resting place,
as above the covers on a hot night.
Studying the carving, I watched
fall slowly as in real time
a single tear, withered lime,
like her face. Liquid, it coursed across her cheek.

These visions belong not to me
but to the faithful, convinced of holy
life in death. And then
the tear was a tiny insect

crossing a mason's work, and not a woman.
Small intruder, you made me look,
startled, alone in the silent nook
with Robine.
I am a skeptic, will be even if I see
a mermaid or a flying rug.
Still, I saw what I saw with fear.
For three seconds it was truly a tear
and only later, a bug.

SILLY DOWN SOUTH

The cat's face a smirk half orange,
half black, divided down the middle—
charmer or vagrant?
The cat's mew a tiny door hinge,
whining just a little—
subtle or flagrant?
The evening star in the day, or is it a plane,
planet, satellite, or rogue?
The accent of this new place far from the main,
damn it, what a wrinkled brogue.
The chef motioned to his assistant,
cue or benediction?
She was food-lorn, fair and distant
with the epicure's affliction.
The white men come and tan, seeking,
speaking and undoing.
The sandpipers run about, beaking,
winging and hallooing.

T U   C L A V E
for Watson

Míramelo, the grandmother
with the small boy instructs (invites) you
to watch her watching him, watch him
for her, watch how good she
feels watching him, watch yourself
next to this child. Grass, confused
by grammar's ambiguity, grows
in all directions. Sun above the park
keeps ticking
yellow as a toy horse.

At the club that night
the cuartos are cold and nobody
knows you're a gringo. Míratelas,
the girls in tight pants and heavy
makeup, like bright emblems
of a grandma's disapproval. Watch
yourself watching them watching you.
Salsa: the sticks keep clicking dos-tres
(the silent unh on the beat before) felt
dancewise, stepwise, and in the throat.

The trumpeter watches his
pal who watches the bandleader who
watches the time. At the back, some old
congueros, grandfathers, watch
nothing; they already know (are familiar
with/conversant in) the language of youth.
Maybe rusty. When Manuel pauses between
songs to wipe his face with his hand
his whiskers sound like a carved gourd,
used to the rhythm, rasping to itself.

SPECIFICITY

Sometimes when we bury our grandparents
we have to locate these old cemeteries in pockets
of Detroit we think should be overgrown, disused, like
a corner of Riga or Kiev, which in fact are well
tended. We have a jar of Petoskey stones to pass around
and we lay them on the ledge one by one.

It's been twenty years since we stood at the pulpit, pointing
a silver finger at animal skin. They taught us so many
syllables for *regret* and *mourn*. We watch our little brothers get
married and our fathers get religious, speaking the same lines
they muttered in Vilna, Sanok and Belz. (There's one photograph
from the thirties where everyone looks scared. Magnesium flash.)

We can still read those pen strokes set in stone, but there is no
more reason. Those who exhorted us are gone and we would
not be tourists in Coval or Volyn. We listen to sermons in
English, if anything, and the third-row yamulka with the block M
reminds us of the Midwestern dream. We always knew
we came from death; we never saw more death coming.

GINKGOS

Put down your fucking phone and attend
to your son, who is grabbing your left hand,
he wants to take this walk (why
I don't have kids, or a smart phone). I watch you
get better as he gets worse; it heartens me how
you lift him, you've dragged yourself out
of the house in those soccer shorts and slides, but he's
dressed for the weather, little man. (I can
remember holding my mother's gloved hand, like her
hand but not her hand, secure as we stepped off a curb
into some yellow leaves. She said, *They're ginkgos,*
she pronounced every letter of that word, I heard the
k and g back to back in my mind.) You're the only father
in the park and that's got to be rough. The women in
abayas don't want to be your friend; the teenagers give
contempt. It's six o'clock and you've been out for hours,
the sky is already lowering, it's October, you're still wearing
your shorts and Vans, and he's still yelling Dad, dad, so you
swing him, fuck the phone and dinner; you're now the only
ones left. You push him as high as he wants to go past full dark.

TWELVE-BAR BLUES

What I love is
an unsentimental river
carrying silt away from
and to

What I love is
an unsentimental river
carrying, oh, silt
away from
and to

What I need is
What I want is
What I fear is
What I'll have is

What I love is an unsentimental
river carrying silt
away from and to.

ELEGY
(EYES OPEN IN THE QUIET)

I perceive an optic silence, valent
the sphere around my head where sound ought be.

Textured shapes accrete on the ceiling, shift
in spectral secrecy, and sway as old
relatives over me, me
in the crib. I coo or cry and fumble into sleep.

I was not alone then, am not now, merely
didn't take stock of the company.

Faces painted between lights and lintels
soar, benevolent; no hands descend
to feel me breathe or rouse me to another age,
passing more than one night's worth of dream.

Where and when? Ceaseless traipse
of traffic only—whatsoever bed or time.

And who watches whom? I let go
my sentinels because their movement was so slow.
If I knew them any, if they love me still, pronounce
this, tacit, words in my dark head: Thank you, I am fine.

PEARL

You remind me of the otherness of persons,
how I can't know you even though I saw you born. I
saw your father born, then I saw him catch you splash and
the twenty-six years between were nothing, a few dinners, a few
exams and jokes. The twenty-six years between were everything. Now
you are here, being everything. I hope to see you old. I like the way we marvel,
foreheads together giddy on the rug. I like the way you fly at me, certain of reception.

WINDOWS OPEN

I'll tell you everything I know about music: birds get
crazy jealous when they hear a flute. Why can't we, they
wonder, spout the three-octave run with flaming tail that
jigs back up, and get our downy bellies pressed
against the piano's cushioned chord? They yelp and spray
haphazard notes, hustle to trees and when they can't compete,
disperse. To practice with the windows open courts little bodies
lobbed through the gaps, against the screen, badminton of
beast-versus-man envy. Creatures trying
a house too big to comprehend.

      Like people hearing poems. I wish I spoke in rhyme.
I'll try my hand at scanning, since hands press keys in time. My
piano student's mom is chopping scallions, it happens, to the Schubert
beat only briefly, then they're chopped, but the measures go on, lieder
longing for accompaniment. Lucy throws herself against it until I coax
her away: let it slide, feel beat three, relax. From the kitchen,
knifeblade sound on the floor. There's no contest with gravity
or meter; they merely are. And like

      hearts hearing about love, a troubadour's myth. It goes
like this. No, like this. How to reconcile what we're equipped with
and what we wanted our talents to be? I'm not a bird. I'm not a cook. I'm
no stringer of pearly words on the stanza line. I can scarcely touch
an instrument, thinking its history. Hardly chat or sing without
wishing better: what I would, with enough breath, range,
and technique for the well-timed twist of phrase, meaning
a modicum of math, sway, and belief in the perfect punchline.
Meaning sympathy for birds small and stupid, for fallible poets
and middle school pianists, the life of damage and want,
fingers and voice going *mine mine.*